The Singing Piano

Book One

By Mark Swope

© 2015 Swope Publications
All Rights Reserved

Acknowledgements

Thank You to all those who contributed their individual time, advice, and expertise. Over the many years it took to research, develop, and produce this series, there have been many wonderful people who have made contributions. I will list many of them here, and others have only been omitted due to my personal shortcomings.

Joe Updegraff, whose technical and musical expertise made this project possible. Thank you for your humor, camaraderie, and support.

Ian Kirk, for your excellent musicianship, and keen attention to detail.

It is wonderful to work with students who are not only interested in learning, but also strive toward making beautiful, musical solutions. Luis Mariscal-Diaz, Abby Thao, Marcus Lawrence, Selena Magallanes, Martha Valencia, Aaron Vang, Jaden Blankenship, Adara Chavez, Rin Le, and Giovanni Granucci.

Professional musicians and educators: Margaret Runaas, Christopher Davis, Anoush Tchakarian, Lydia Megale.

SP-5001
© 2015 Swope Publications
www.thesingingpiano.com

ISBN #978-1-7323086-0-2

Distributed by Swope Publications
5049 C Pacific Avenue, Stockton, CA 95207

International copyright secured. All rights reserved. Printed in the United States of America. No portion of this book may be reproduced, stored in a retrieval system, or transmitted in any form or means - mechanical, photocopying, recording, or other - without prior permission.

Printed in the United States of America.

CONTENTS

Introduction 2
Lesson 1: Sets of Two Black Keys 4
Lesson 2: Sets of Three Black Keys 6
Lesson 3: White Keys 7
Lesson 4: Repeated Notes 9
Lesson 5: Notes Moving Up 11
Lesson 6: Notes Moving Down 12
Lesson 7: Moving Down & Up 13
Lesson 8: Using Multiple Fingers 14
    Reflection in my Tea 17
Lesson 9: Five Finger Pattern 18
    Race Horse Racing 19
    Surfing the Internet 20
    Ode To Joy 21
Lesson 10: Note Names & Changing Fingers 22
    Riding The Wind (primo) 24
    Riding The Wind (secundo) 25
Lesson 11: Ties & Patterns 26
    Bucket of Tears 27
Lesson 12: Dynamics 28
    Gesu Bambino 29
    Remembering My Password 30
Lesson 13: DRM Tonal Solfege (major tonality) 31
Lesson 14: Major Tonality Melodies 33
Lesson 15: DRM Notation 34
    186,000mps (DRM) 36
Lesson 16: Grand Staff 37
    #Rainbows (DRM) 38
    Strudel (DRM) 39
    Theme & Variation (DRM) 40
Lesson 17: Treble & Bass Clefs 41
Lesson 18: LTD Tonal Solfege (minor tonality) 42
    Red Light, Green Light (LTD) 43
    I Lost My Shoe (LTD) 43
Lesson 19: Minor Solfege Melodies 44
    Rose Thorn, Why Do You Scorn? (LTD) 44
    Mushy Cereal (LTDR) 44
Lesson 20: LTD Notation 45
    March of the Elephants (LTD) 45

APPENDIX A: Major Pentachords 46
APPENDIX B: Minor Pentachords 47

INTRODUCTION (music readiness)

1. "My Body is My Instrument"

You can't make music without your body. Take good care of it. Feed it. Move it. Clean it. Take it out to play. Put it away at the end of the day.

2. Breathing...

...sustains life and music notes. Breathing affects the body, its movement, how much it can lift, how fast it can run, how anxious it feels, and how calmly it rests. Gently and silently breath in through the nose; exhaling gently and silently through the mouth. Remember to breath.

3. Posture...

...allows the body to be ready. Keep your head tall and shoulders relaxed. Sitting on the front half of the piano bench, touch the front edge of the white keys with the tips of your middle fingers. Adjust the bench and your body so that your elbows are at your sides in this position. When your hands and fingers move onto the keys, elbows should be slightly forward. Keep legs side by side (not crossed at the knees nor ankles).

4. Wrists...

...must be level and flexible, and should "float" with the arm and hand comfortably. Piano playing involves the body, arms, wrists, and fingers working together. Any pain or discomfort is an indication that a change in approach is needed. Hold both hands up and rotate them as if you are gently changing a lightbulb. This light, relaxed, rotating feeling is similar to the one you should have while playing.

5. Fingers...

...are naturally curved. Not straight and not like a claw. Turn your hands palms up with fingers naturally curved as if you are holding a soccer ball in each hand. Now turn your hands, palms down, placing all five fingers on the keyboard. Place one finger on each white key. This is a *Five Finger Position*. Make sure all fingers are resting on the keys, including the thumb and pinky.

6. Playing...

...starts with the body, requires a breath, is strengthened by posture readiness, and moves through flexible wrists and capable fingers. Comfortably move the arm to support the fingers as they play. Keep all fingers close to the keys. Breath. Listen.

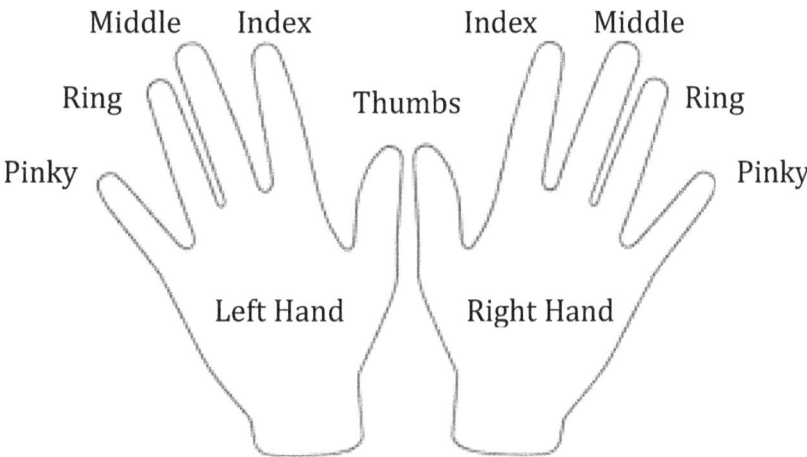

LESSON 1 (sets of two black keys)

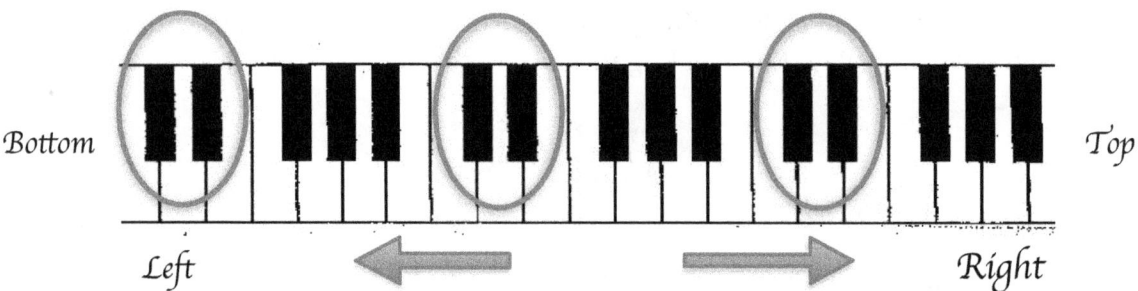

Use two left hand fingers  to play the set of two black keys closest to the

bottom of the keyboard simultaneously (as the same time). Play each set of two black keys

moving up the keyboard to the right.

When you reach the center of the keyboard directly in front of your body, switch to using

two right hand fingers  and continue playing each set of two black keys

until you reach the top.

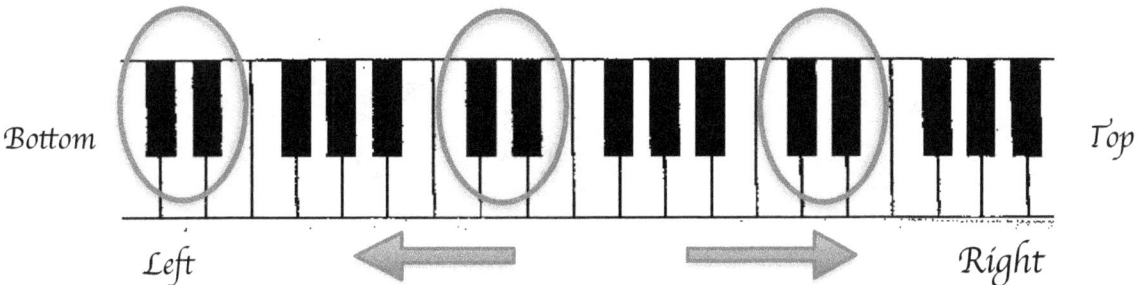

Use two right hand fingers  to play the set of two black keys closest to the top of the keyboard simultaneously (as the same time). Play each set of two black keys moving down the keyboard to the left.

When you reach the center of the keyboard directly in front of your body, switch to using two left hand fingers  and continue playing each set of two black keys until you reach the bottom.

Repeat this process moving up and down the keyboard freely. Remember to breath.

LESSON 2 (sets of three black keys)

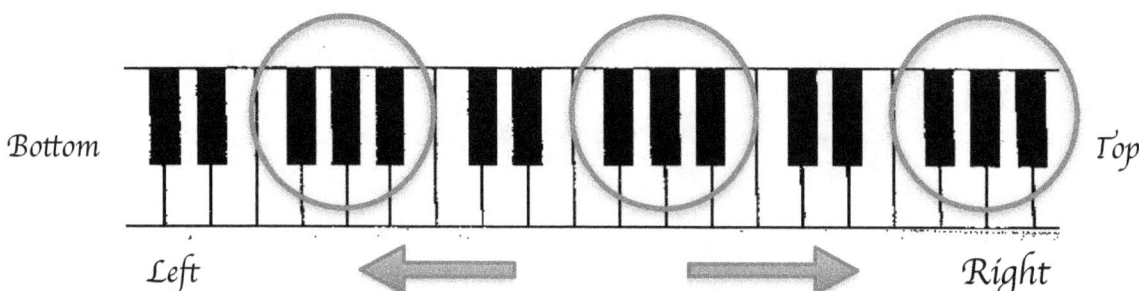

 Use three left hand fingers to play the set of three black keys closest to the bottom of the keyboard simultaneously (at the same time). Play each set of three black keys moving up the keyboard to the right.

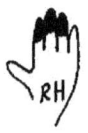 When you reach the center of the keyboard directly in front of your body, switch to using three right hand fingers and continue playing each set of three black keys until you reach the top.

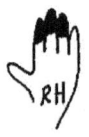 Use three right hand fingers to play the set of three black keys closest to the top of the keyboard simultaneously (at the same time). Play each set of three black keys moving down the keyboard to the left.

 When you reach the center of the keyboard directly in front of your body, switch to using three left hand fingers and continue playing each set of three black keys until you reach the bottom.

Repeat this process moving up and down the keyboard freely.

Remember to breathe.

LESSON 3 (white keys)

1. Use this finger  to play this white key

2. Play this key starting at the bottom of the keyboard. Moving this way ➝ play this key each time it appears until you reach the top. Playing the same key, start at the top of the keyboard. Moving this way ⟵ play this key each time it appears until you reach the bottom.

3. Play the song **Stormy Day** with your teacher. Use this finger  to play this key  Play until the music feels like it is going to end.

Teacher: play in any octave

1. How many sets of two black keys are there?
2. How many sets of three black keys are there?

3. What are the finger names?

1st Challenge: Play using a different finger.
2nd Challenge: Play using a left hand finger.
3rd Challenge: Play the same key in a different location (your teacher may need to move)

7

4. Use this finger 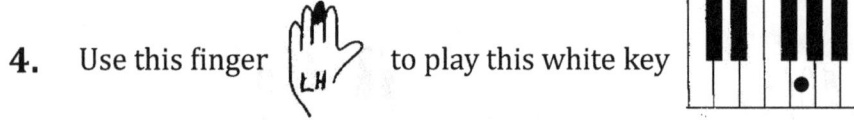 to play this white key

5. Play this key starting at the bottom of the keyboard. Moving this way ➡ play this key each time it appears until you reach the top. Playing the same key, start at the top of the keyboard. Moving this way ⬅ play this key each time it appears until you reach the bottom.

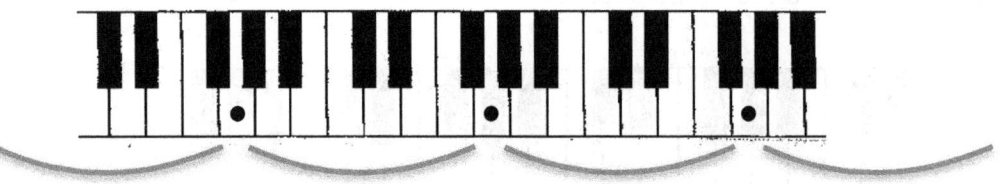

6. To play the song **Skipping** use this finger 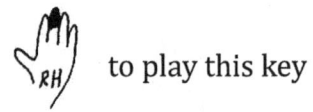 to play this key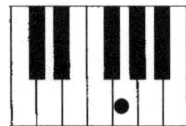

with your teacher. Play until the music feels like it is going to end.

Accompaniment   Teacher: play in any octave

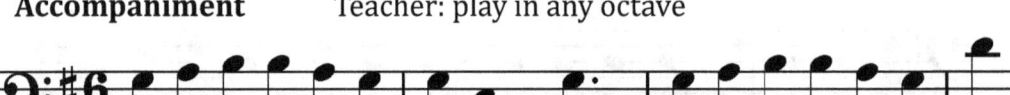

1st Challenge: Play *Stormy Day* using a different finger.
2nd Challenge: Play *Stormy Day* using a left hand finger.
3rd Challenge: Your teacher will choose a white key. Find all of the same key moving up and down the keyboard.

LESSON 4 (repeated notes)

1. Use this finger ✋ to play this key 🎹 shown by this note 𝅗𝅥

Each note is played using a steady **beat**, or *macrobeat*. The macrobeat is shown by the Beat Bar below the first notes of each line. Always use excellent hand position.

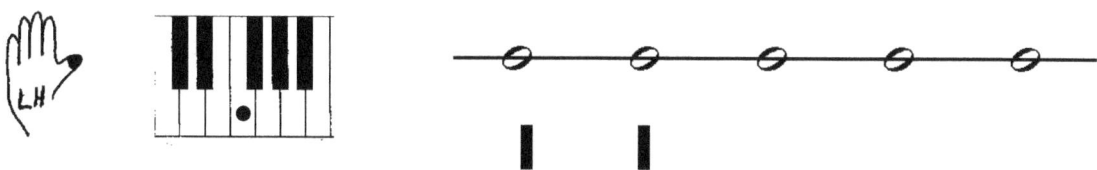

2. Sometimes Dotted White Notes receive the macrobeat. Remember to breath.

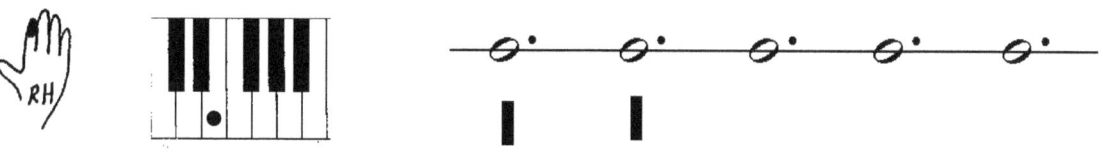

Try playing this exercise with a left hand finger.

3. Using Black Notes as the macrobeat works the same way.

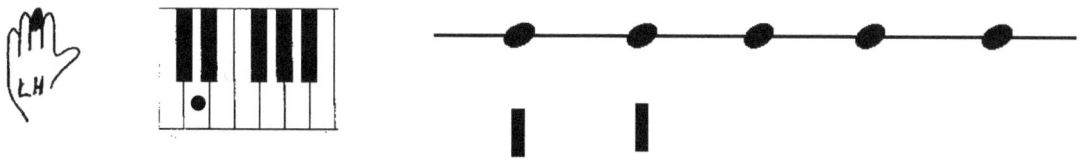

Try playing this exercise with a right hand finger.

4. Sometimes Dotted Black Notes receive the macrobeat.

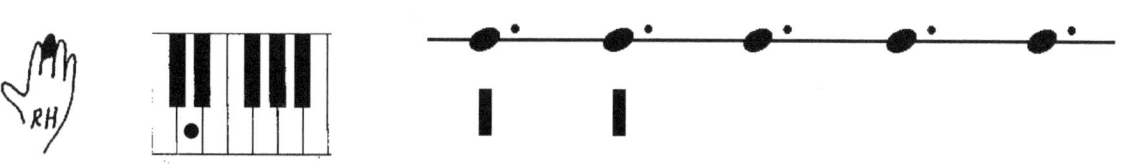

Try playing this exercise with a left hand finger.

5. Changing fingers. On one key, play each note using a different finger as shown. Maintain a steady macrobeat.

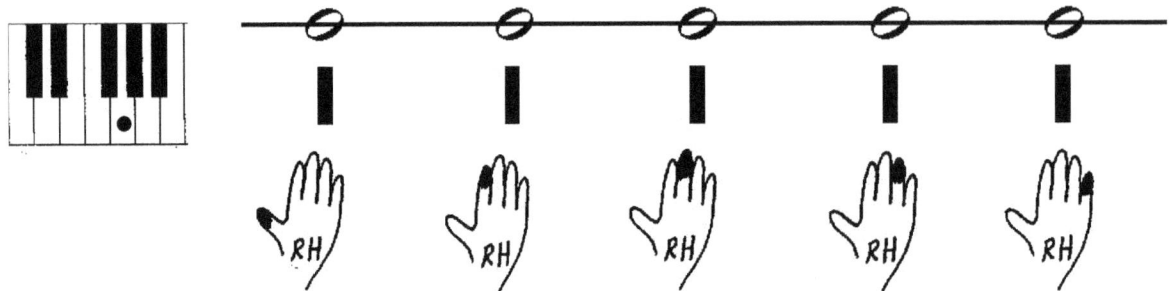

6. Using a Dotted Black Note in the space below the line works the same way!

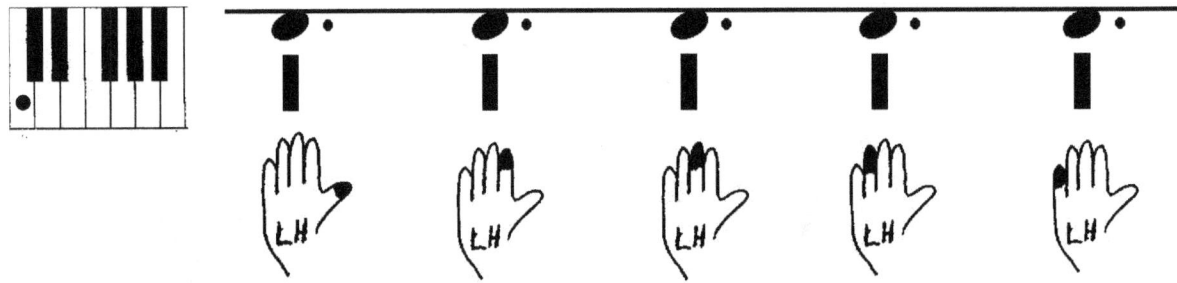

7. Dotted White Notes in the space between lines.

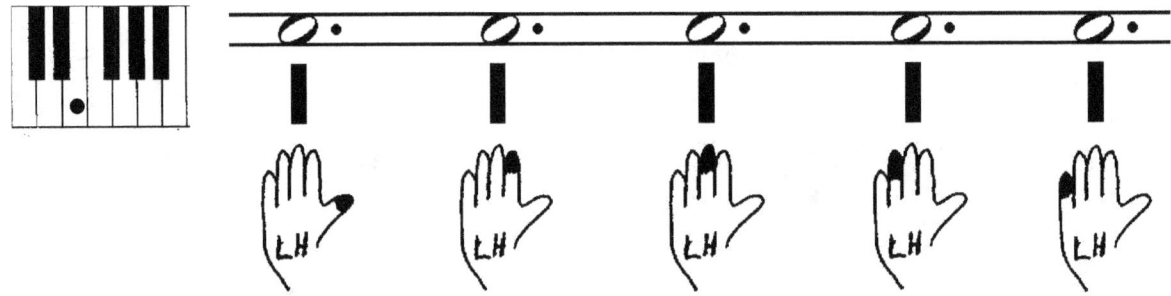

8. Black Notes on the line.

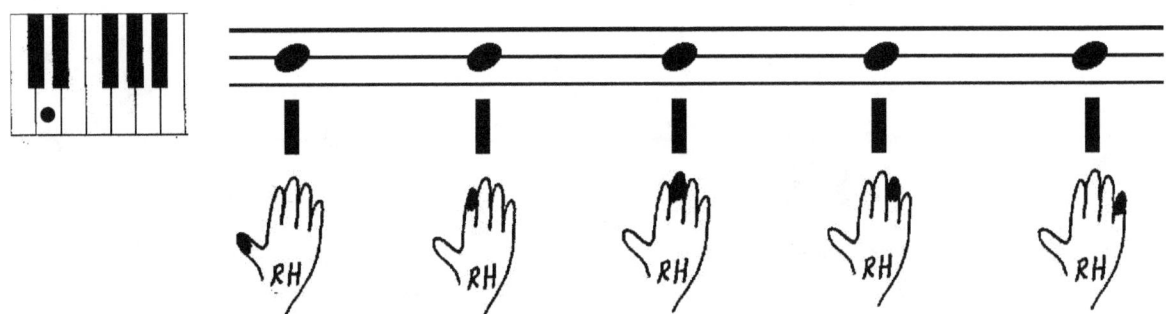

LESSON 5 (notes moving up)

Staff – The five lines and four spaces on which notes are written.

Line notes on the staff   Space notes on the staff

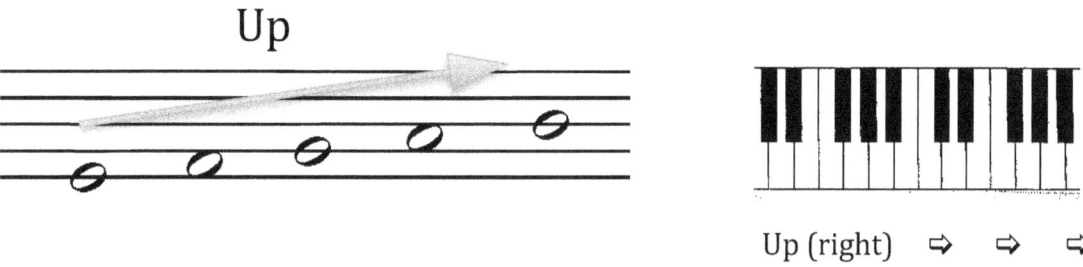

When notes on the staff move up, the hand moves up (to the right) on the keyboard.

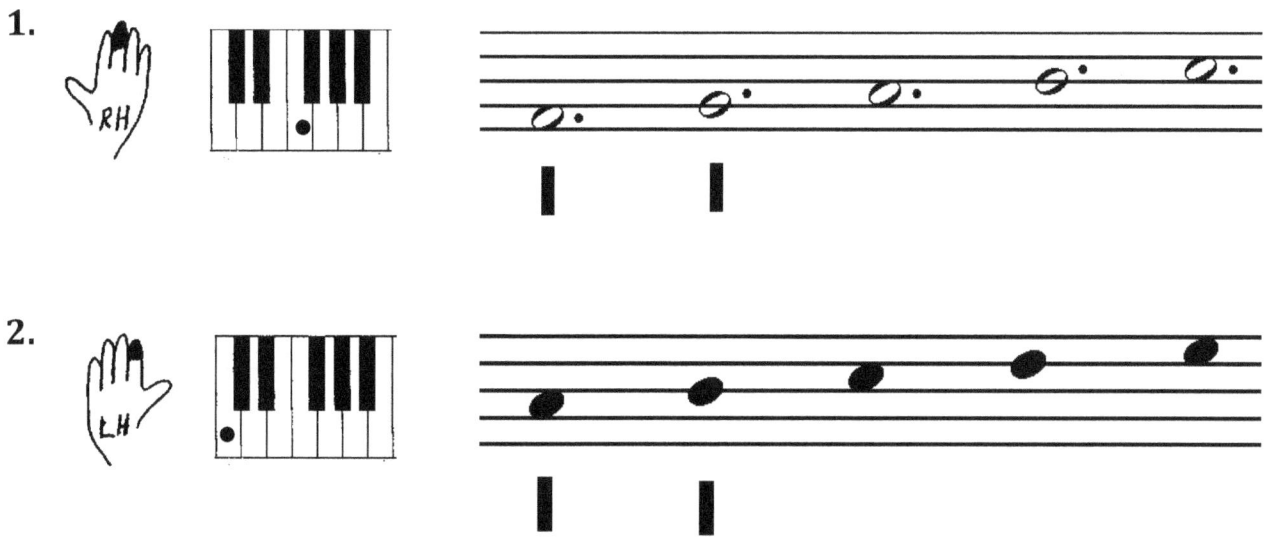

Each line or space note on the staff is the next white key on the keyboard.

Play the following exercises using only the finger shown. The key shown is the first note on the staff. Your hand will move up (to the right) with each note.

1.

2.

11

LESSON 6 (notes moving down)

When notes on the **staff** move down, the hand moves down (to the left) on the keyboard.

Each line or space on the staff represents a white key on the keyboard.

Use only the finger indicated to play the exercise. The key shown is the first note on the staff. Your hand will move to the left (down) with each note. Use excellent playing technique.

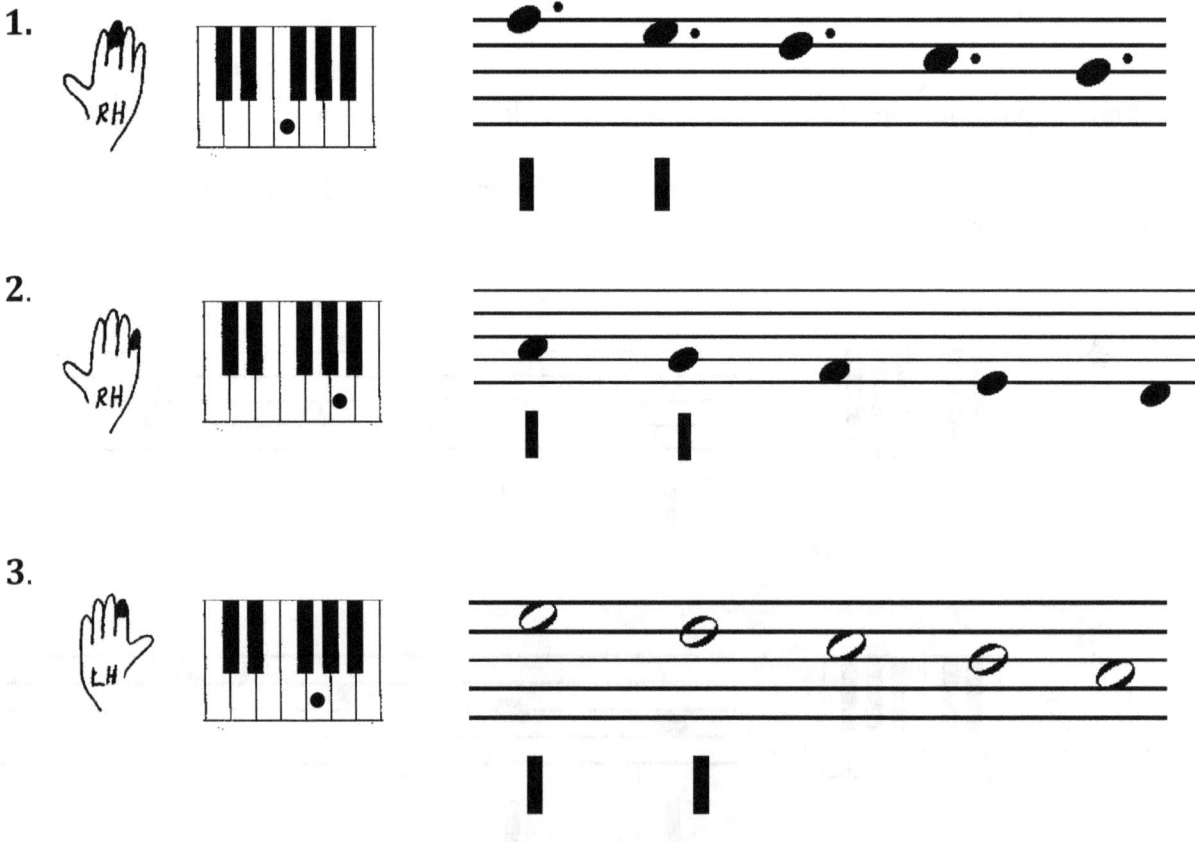

12

LESSON 7 (moving down and up)

Play the following exercises using only the finger shown. When notes move DOWN on the staff, move your hand LEFT to the next white key. When notes move UP on the staff, move your hand RIGHT to the next white key. Start where shown on the keyboard, and use the finger indicated. Try each exercise using a different finger. Always use excellent playing technique and a steady beat.

1. Music will generally have the same number of macrobeats in each measure. How many macrobeats are there here?

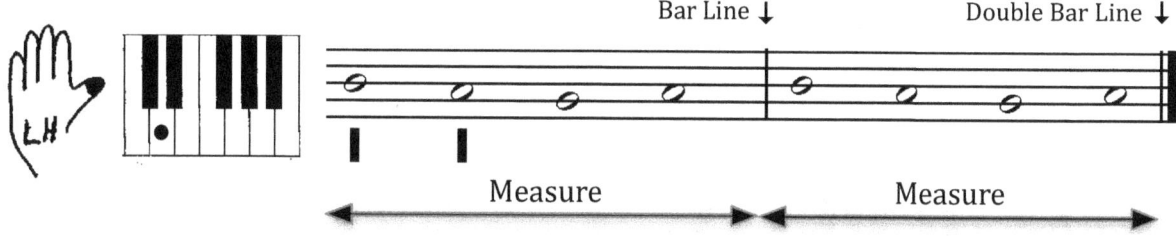

2. How many beats in each measure? How many measures? Try using the Index Finger.

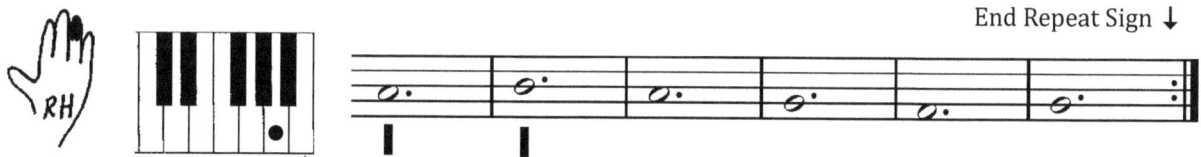

End Repeat Sign - means go back to the beginning.

3. How many measures without the repeat? How many measure with the repeat?

4. How many measures? How many beats in each measure? Try using the Ring Finger.

LESSON 8 (using multiple fingers)

Five-finger Position - When all five fingers are placed on each consecutive white key. All five fingers may not be used.

Play using the fingers shown and start with the finger indicated on the given key. Play each exercise several times until comfortable and easy. Use a steady macrobeat. Your hand will remain in a five-finger position and will not move left nor right.

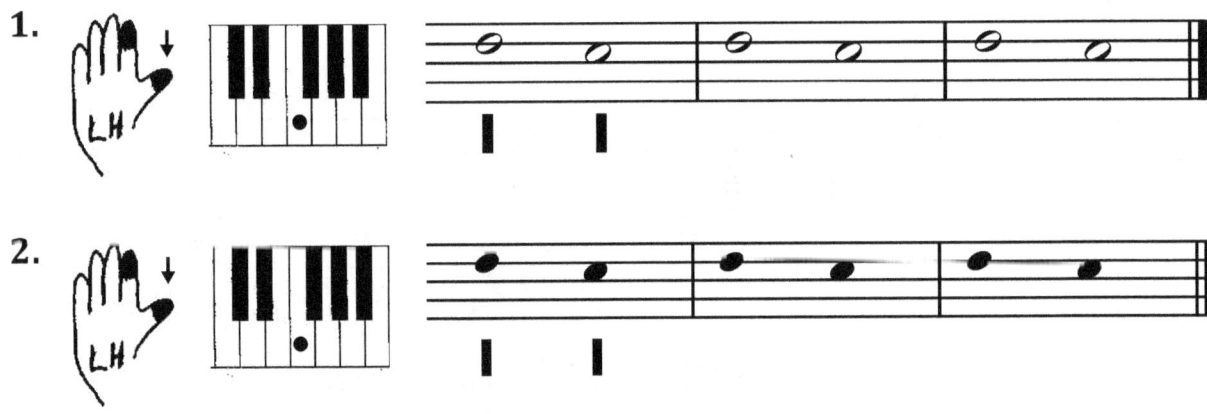

Do lines 1 and 2 **look** the same or different?
Do lines 1 and 2 **sound** the same or different?

Challenge: Play line 1 using different left hand fingers.

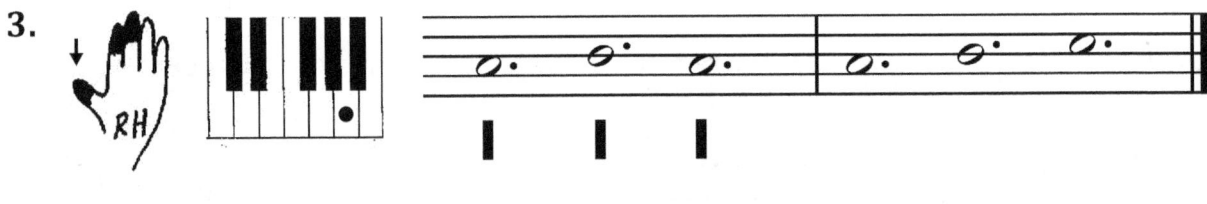

Do lines 3 and 4 **look** the same or different?
Do lines 3 and 4 **sound** the same or different?

Challenge: Play line 4 using different right hand fingers.

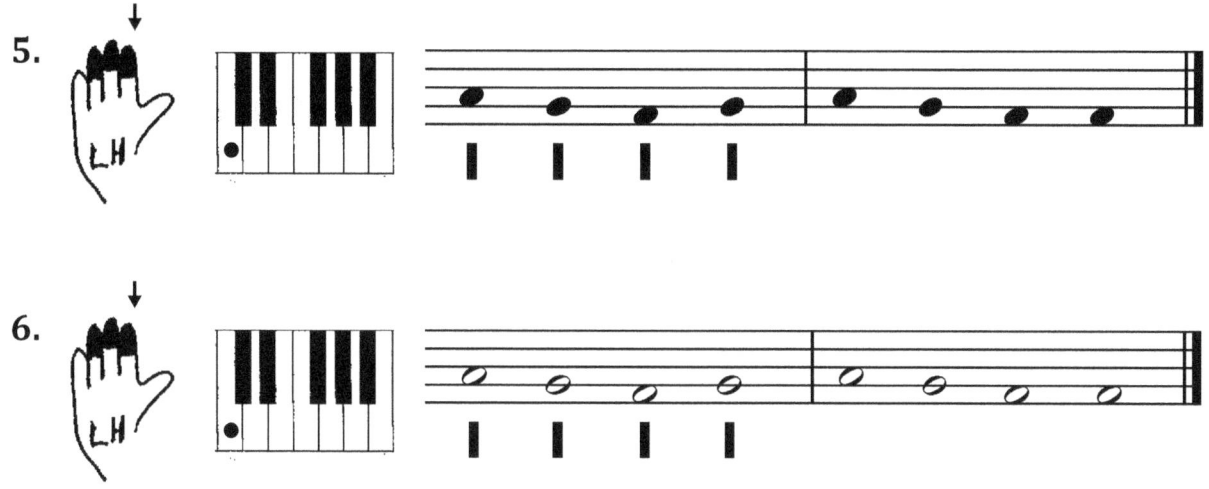

Do lines 5 and 6 **look** the same or different?
Do lines 5 and 6 **sound** the same or different?

1st Challenge: Play line 5 with your right hand. Which fingers will you use?
2nd Challenge: Play line 6 again using the same starting key in a higher or lower location.

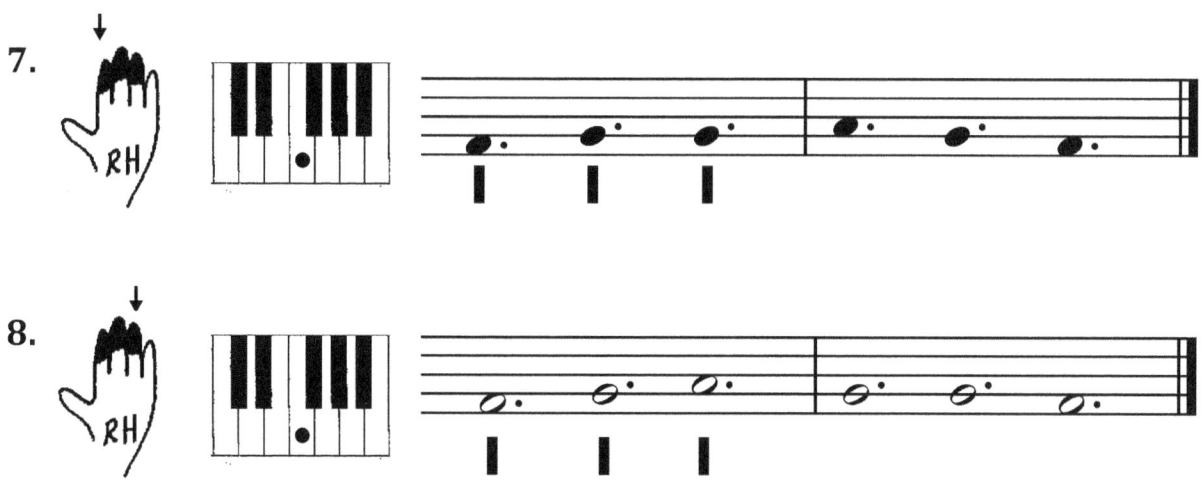

Do lines 7 and 8 **look** the same or different?
Do lines 7 and 8 **sound** the same or different?

1st Challenge: Play line 7 with your left hand. Which fingers will you use?
2nd Challenge: Play line 8 again using the same starting key in a higher or lower location.

> ***Tempo*** - the speed or mood of music being played.
> The tempo indicates how fast or slow the macrobeat is to move,
> and can also indicate the mood or feeling of a piece.
> *Tempi* or *Tempos*, plural.

Reflection In My Tea
Teacher Accompaniment

Mark Swope

Walking

Reflection In My Tea (title)

 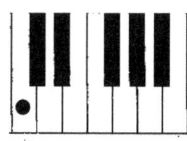

Start with the right hand thumb on the key shown. That key is the first note on the staff.

Walking (tempo/mood)　　　　　　　　　　　　　　　　　Mark Swope (composer)

↓ Rest (Silence)

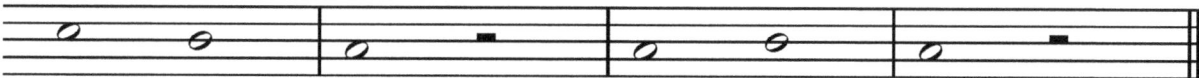

1. What is the title?
2. Who is the composer?
3. What is the tempo or mood?
4. How many macrobeats in each measure?
5. Does each measure have the same number of beats?

1st Challenge: Play using different right hand fingers.
2nd Challenge: Sing along using "loo" as you play.
3rd Challenge: Play the same song as if the title were "Shark Attack!" How is it different from "Reflection in My Tea?"
4th Challenge: Add microbeat rhythms.

LESSON 9 (five finger pattern)

Use a *five-finger pattern* to play each exercise several times until comfortable and easy. Keep a steady macrobeat. Using all five fingers, your hand will stay over the same five white keys.

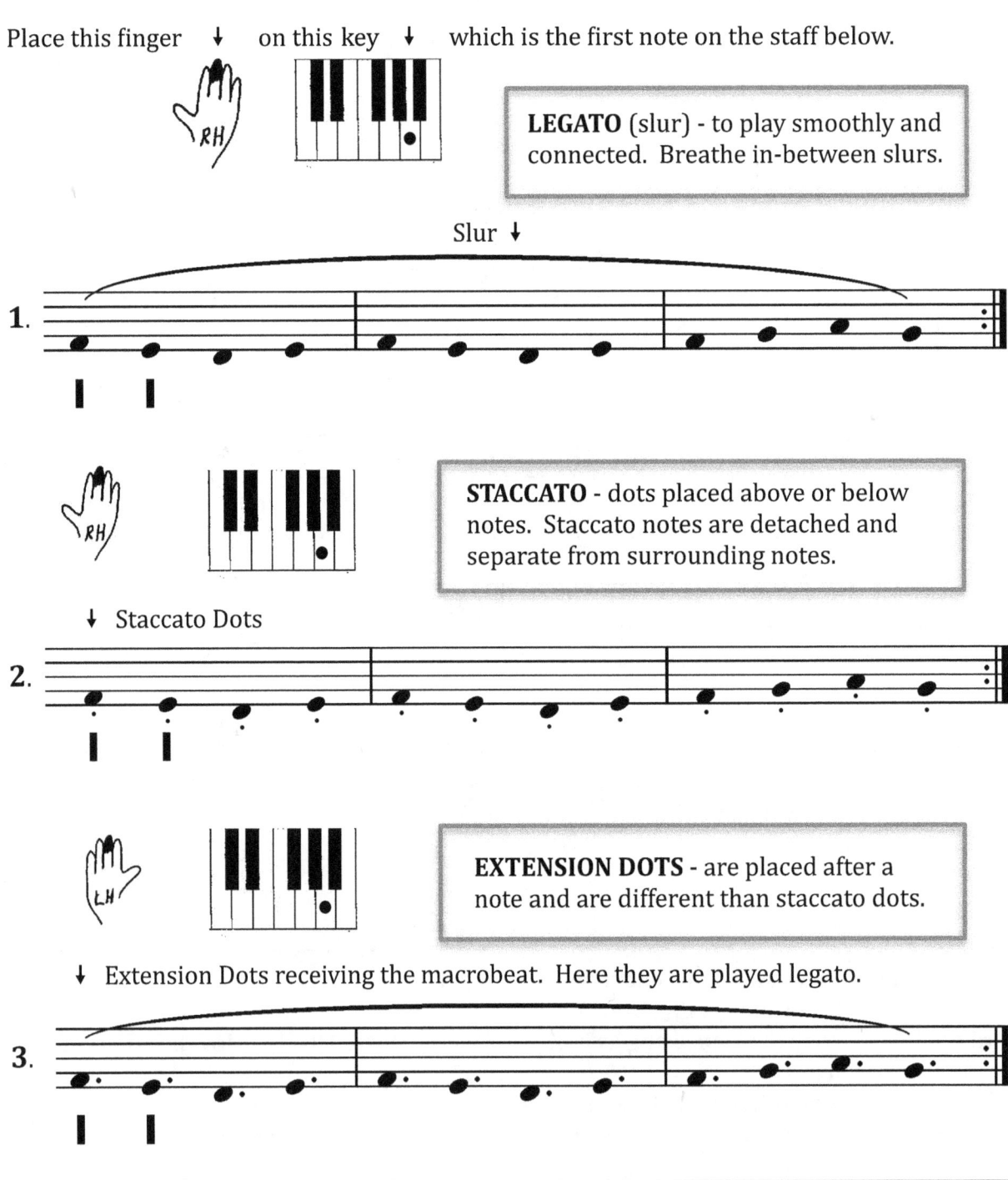

1st Challenge: Play #1 in a different location.
2nd Challenge: Play #2 with your left hand. What finger will you start with?

> **ARTICULATION** - how a note is played. **Staccato** and **legato** are articulations. Generally, piano music is played legato unless indicated.

 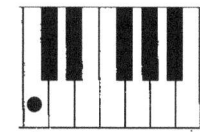 _Race Horse Racing_ (title)

Fast (tempo/mood)　　　　　　　　　　　　　　　　　　Mark Swope (composer)

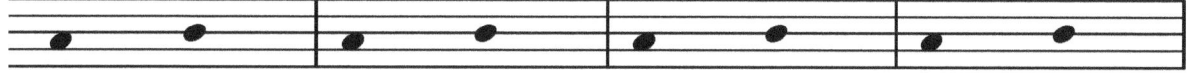

↓ Rest

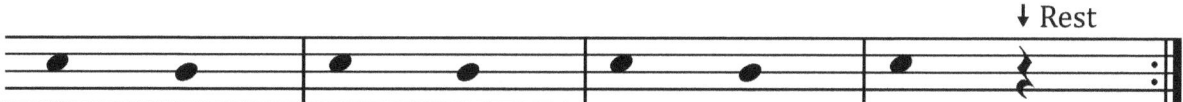

Repeat Sign (to the beginning) ↑

1st Challenge: Play staccato.
2nd Challenge: Play with your right hand.
3rd Challenge: Play as if the title were "Race Turtle Racing!" How is it different?
4th Challenge: Play again starting on the same key but a different location.

Teacher: Play below student or above student.

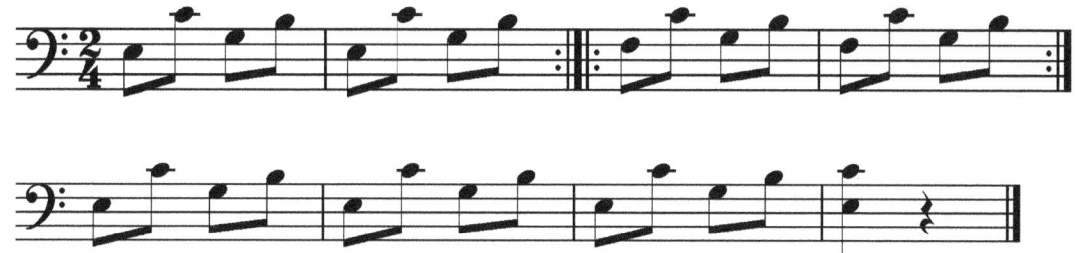

19

Surfing the Internet

  Play using all five fingers

Moderately Slow   Mark Swope

1. What is the title?
2. Who is the composer?
3. How many beats in each measure?
4. Does each measure have the same number of beats?
5. What articulation is used?

1st Challenge: Play using the same starting key in a different location.
2nd Challenge: Play starting with your right hand middle finger.
3rd Challenge: Use two hands playing simultaneously.
4th Challenge: Play using microbeat rhythms.

Ode To Joy
from Ninth Symphony

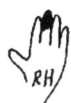 

Ludwig van Beethoven (1770 - 1827)
arranged by Mark Swope

 Joyfully

(unresolved ending)

(resolved ending)

1. What is the title?
2. Who is the composer?
3. Who is the arranger?
4. What is the tempo or mood?
5. When did Beethoven live?
6. The A Sections are mostly the same. What is different?

1st Challenge: Play legato starting with the left hand middle finger.
2nd Challenge: Play in a different location.
3rd Challenge: Play hands together.
4th Challenge: Play staccato.

LESSON 10 (Note Names & Changing Fingers)

Stems - note stems can go UP on the right side of the note head, or DOWN on the left side of the note head. Stems don't change how a note is performed.

Play the following exercises using *five-finger patterns*. Place the finger indicated on the key provided. That key is the starting note of each exercise. Play each exercise several times until easy and comfortable. Make sure to change fingers when indicated, including on the repeat.

QUARTER NOTE

| Quarter Note (Stem Up) | Quarter Note (Stem Down) | Quarter Rest (Silence) |

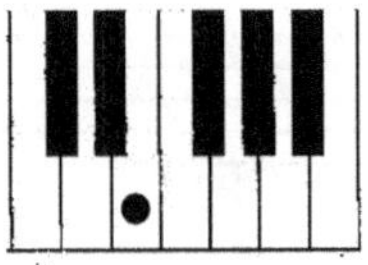

1. Quarter Note Macrobeat.
    Challenge: Add simple meter microbeat rhythms.

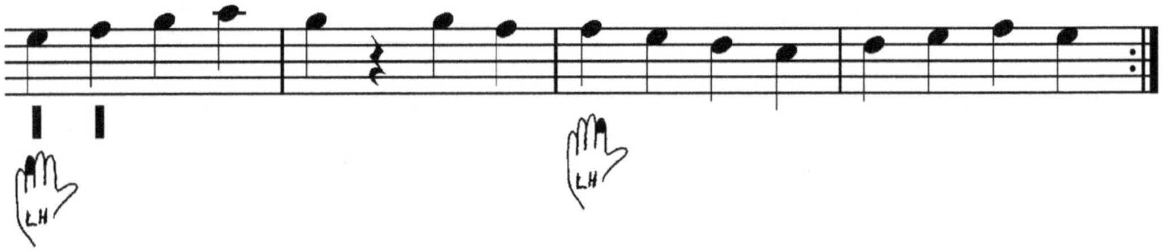

HALF NOTE

| Half Note (Stem Up) | Half Note (Stem Down) | Half Rest (Silence) |

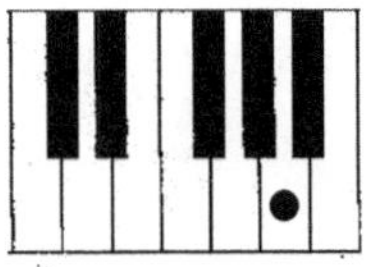

2. Quarter Note Macrobeat.
    Challenge: Add simple meter microbeat rhythms.

DOTTED QUARTER NOTE

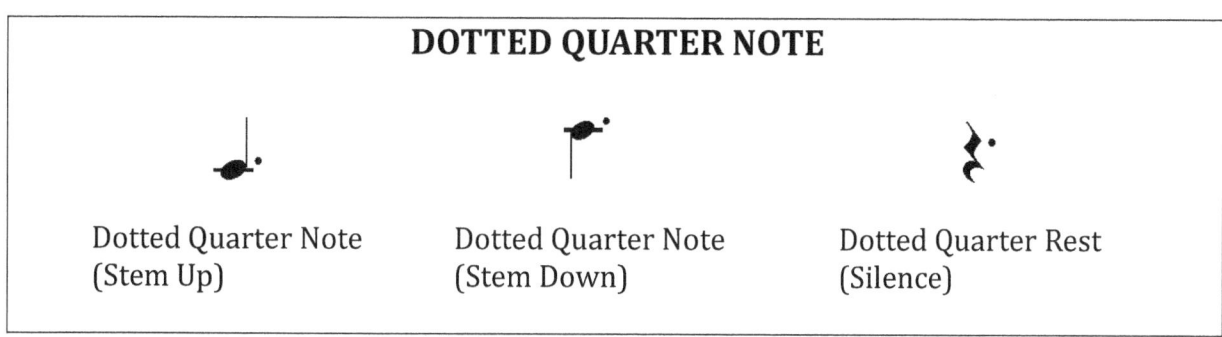

Dotted Quarter Note (Stem Up) Dotted Quarter Note (Stem Down) Dotted Quarter Rest (Silence)

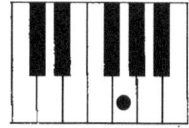

3. Dotted Quarter Note Macrobeat.
   Challenge: Add compound meter microbeat rhythms.

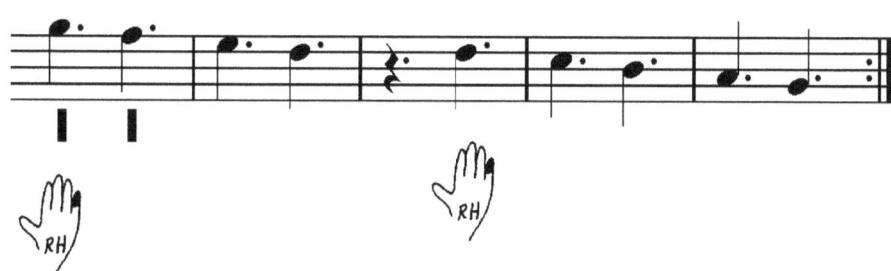

DOTTED HALF NOTE

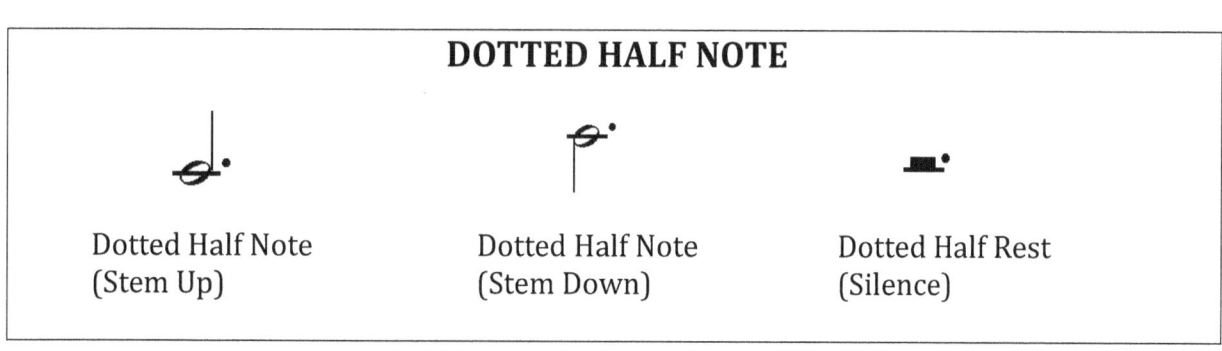

Dotted Half Note (Stem Up) Dotted Half Note (Stem Down) Dotted Half Rest (Silence)

4. Dotted Half Note Macrobeat.
   Challenge: Add compound meter microbeat rhythms.

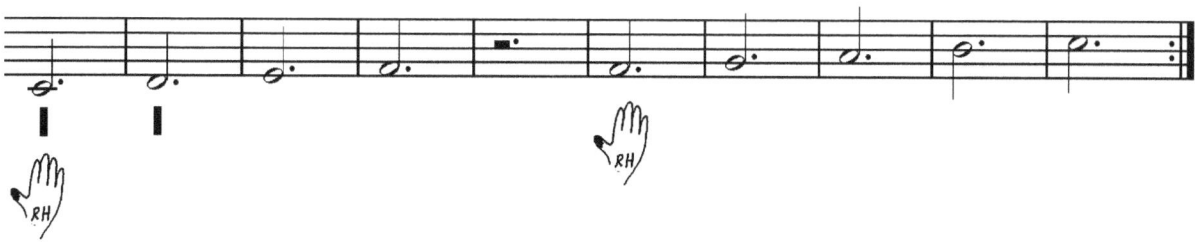

Riding the Wind (secundo)
(Quarter Note Macrobeat)

Mark Swope

Score Analysis:
1. What is the title?
2. Who is the composer?
3. What is the form of this piece?
4. What kind of note receives the macrobeat?

1st Challenge: Play using microbeat rhythms.
2nd Challenge: Play using the left hand. What finger will you start with?

LESSON 11 (ties & patterns)

Tie - when the rhythmic value of two notes is combined. Ties are shown by a slur between two notes on the same line or space.

These tied notes are to be held for two macrobeats.

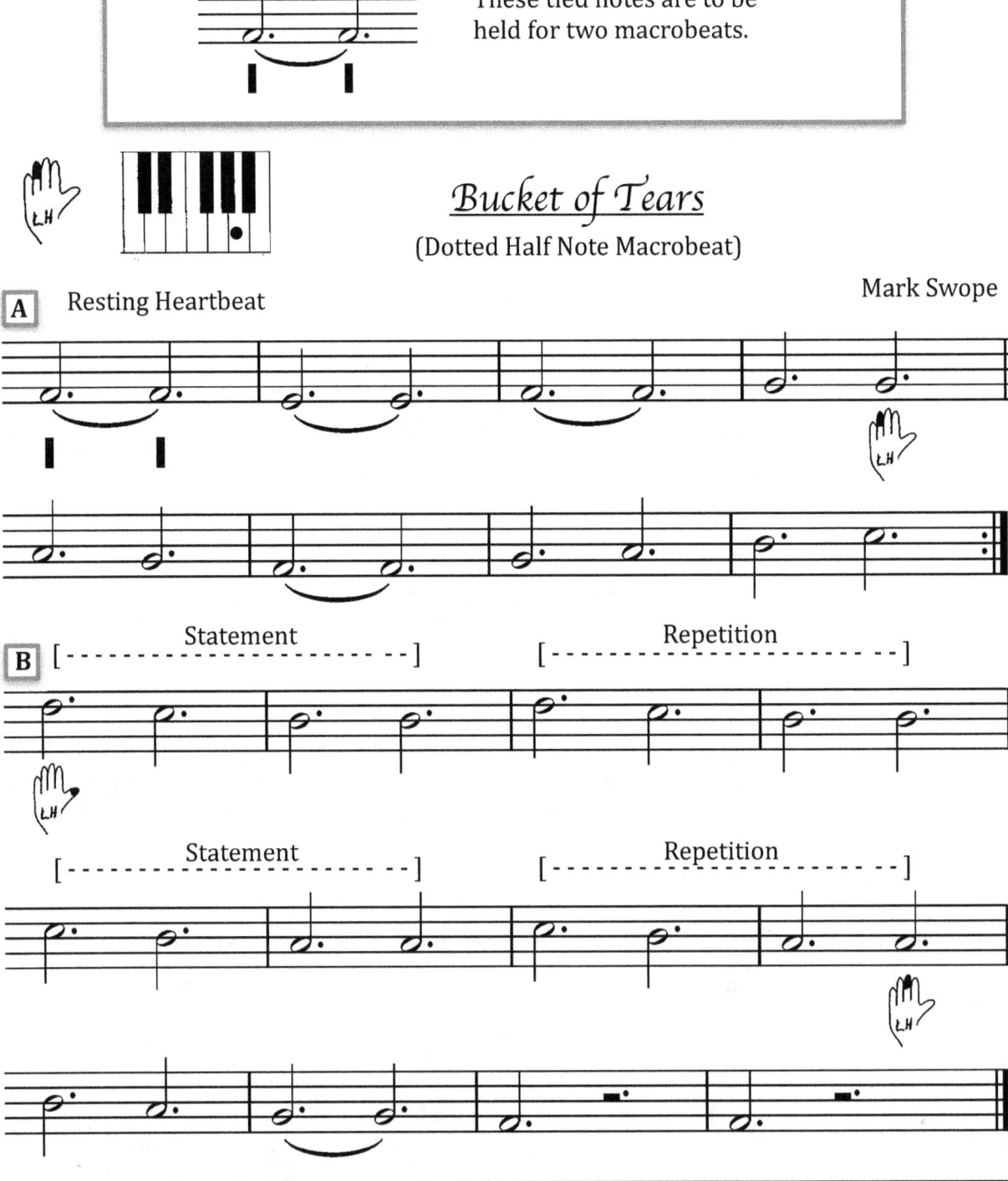

Bucket of Tears
(Dotted Half Note Macrobeat)

Mark Swope

1st Challenge: Play each "Pattern" strong and each "Repetition" soft. Include Section A.
2nd Challenge: Play using the right hand. What finger will you start with?

26

Bucket of Tears
accompaniment

Resting Heartbeat

Mark Swope

Score Analysis:
1. What is the title?
2. Who is the composer?
3. What is the mood or tempo?
4. How many macrobeats in each measure?
5. What kind of note receives the macrobeat?
6. Was the song played legato or staccato?

Challenge: Play using microbeat rhythms.

LESSON 12 (dynamics)

Dynamics – Volume. An indication of how loud or soft music is to be performed.

Symbol	Italian	Translation	Relative Volume Level
pp	Pianissimo	Very Soft	1
p	Piano	Soft	2
mp	Mezzo-Piano	Medium Soft	4
mf	Mezzo-Forte	Medium Strong	6
f	Forte	Strong	8
ff	Fortissimo	Very Strong	10

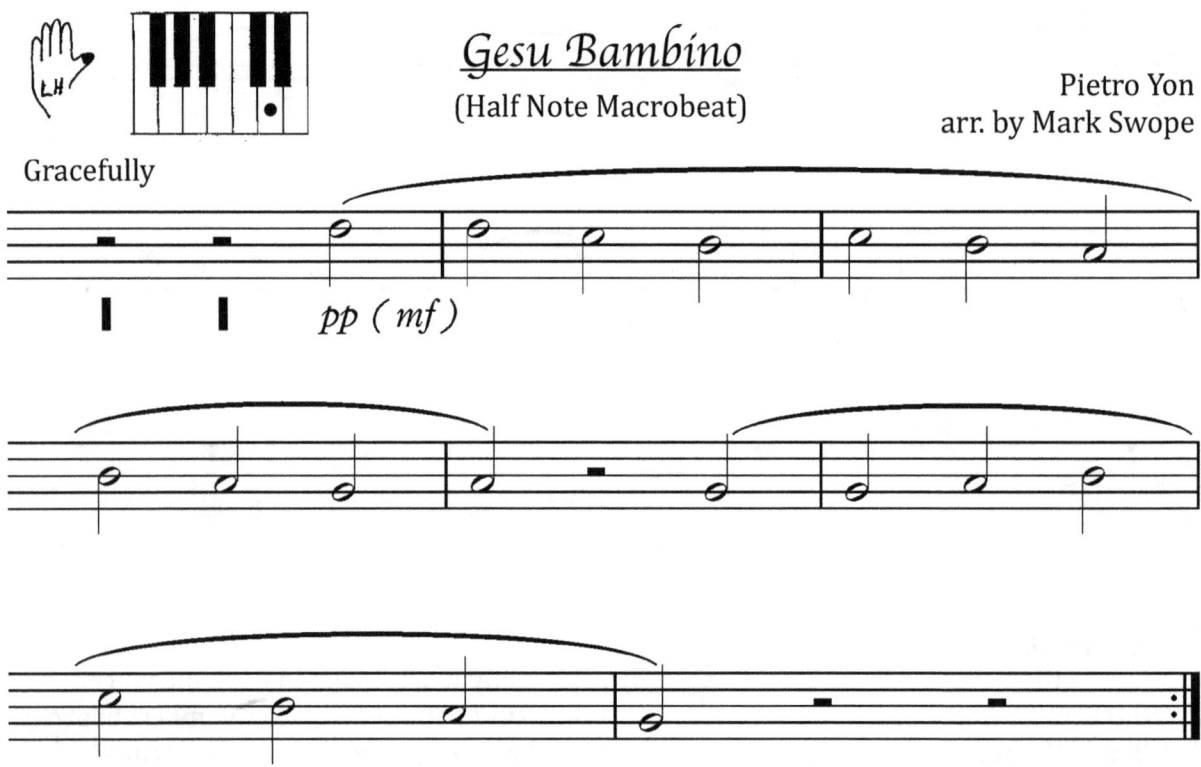

Gesu Bambino
(Half Note Macrobeat)

Pietro Yon
arr. by Mark Swope

Gracefully

pp (mf)

1st Challenge: Play with the right hand in a high location.
2nd Challenge: Play staccato and pianissimo.
3rd Challenge: Play hands together and legato.

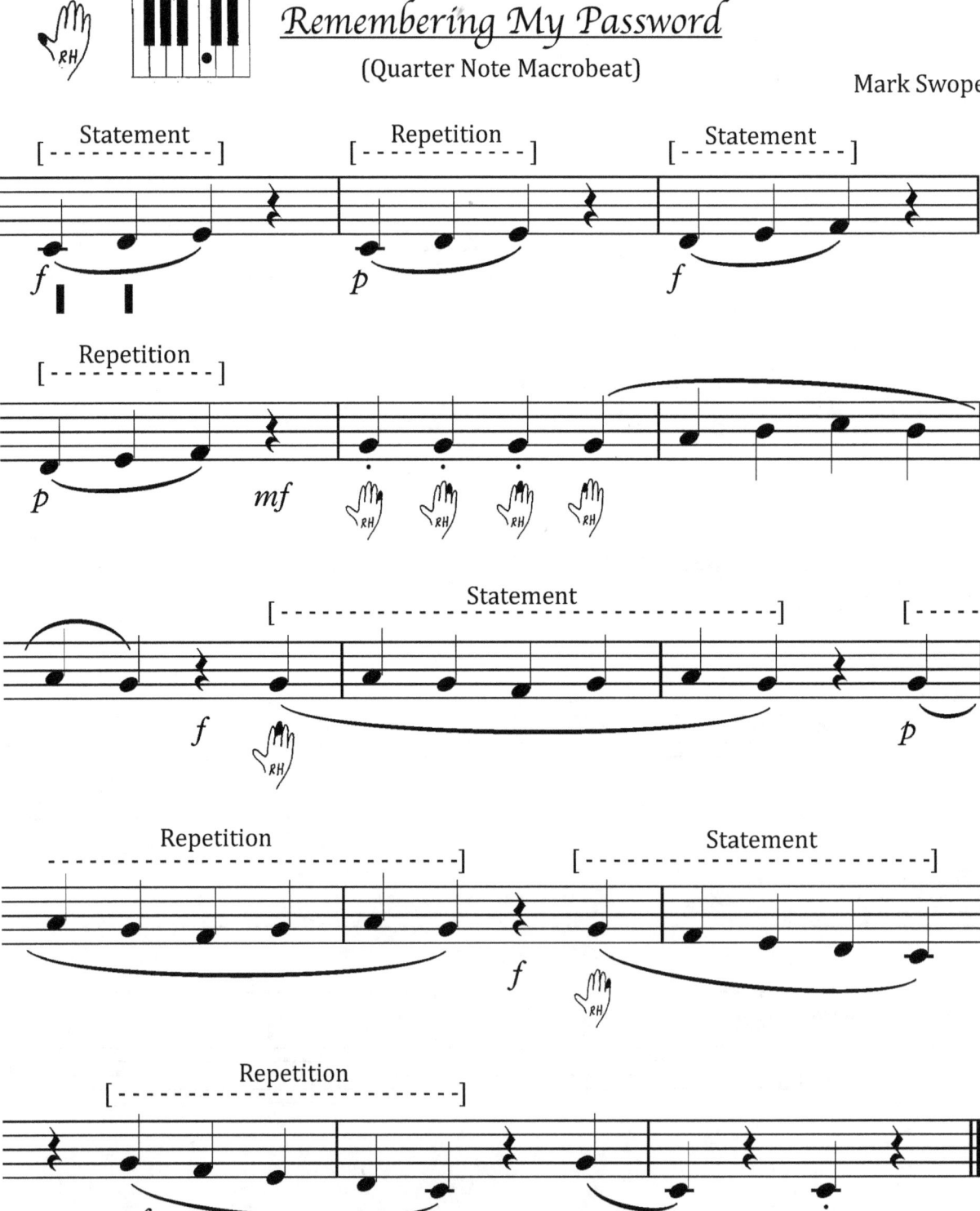

LESSON 13 (DRM tonal solfege)

Tonal Solfege (SOHL-fej) - a system of syllables (DO RE MI FA SO LA TI DO) used to facilitate music reading, pattern recognition, and music understanding.

DO (Doh) - one starting tone in solfege. DO can be the *resting tone*, or *tonic*. Because DO can be moved to any key on the keyboard, this system is called Moveable DO. Music notation will always indicate which key is DO.

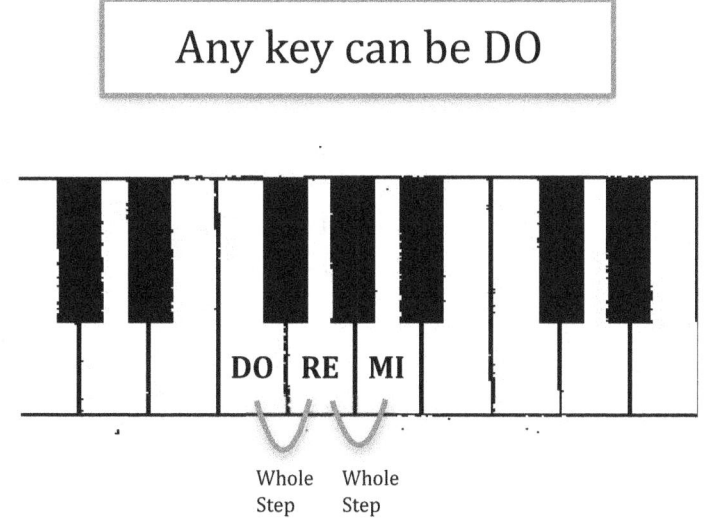

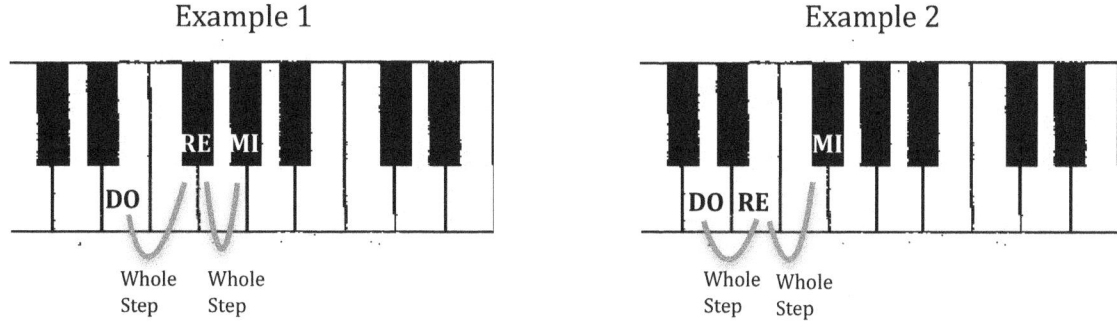

Play DRM starting on the DO provided.
Use different sets of left hand and right hand fingers.

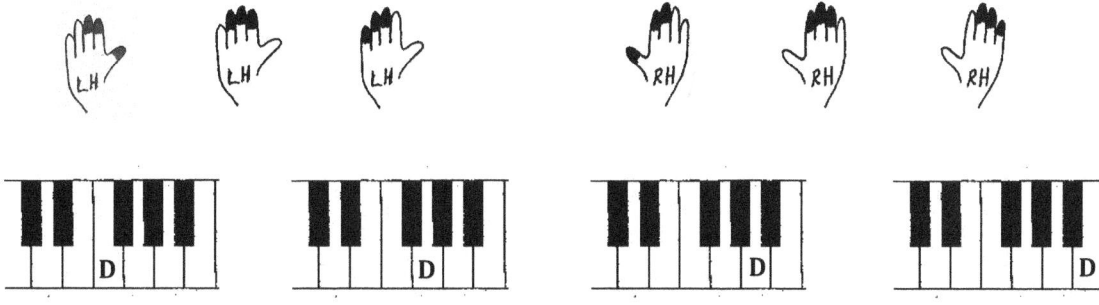

Using three fingers and the keys shown, play solfege patterns. Keep a steady macrobeat and excellent hand position.

1.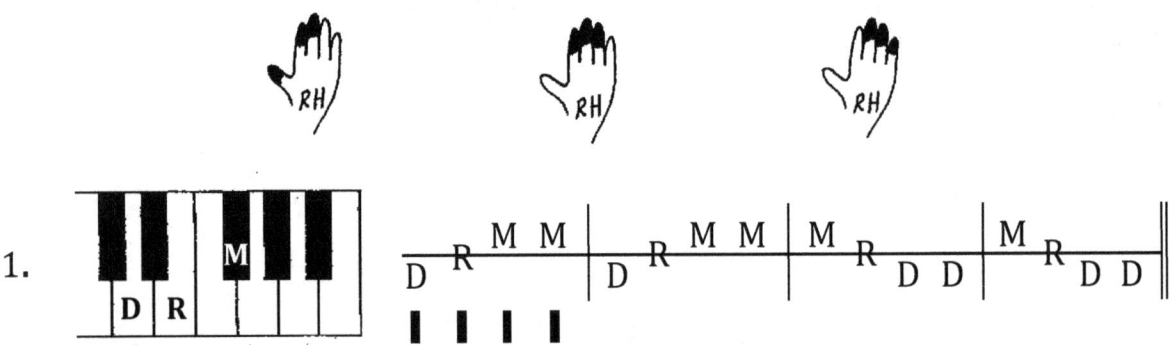

Retrograde - when a music pattern is written in reverse order. Below, the second line is the reverse of the first line.

2.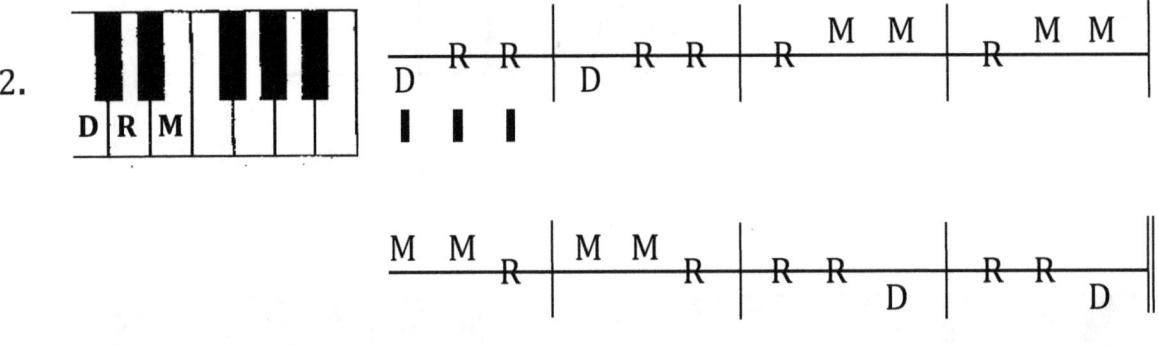

3.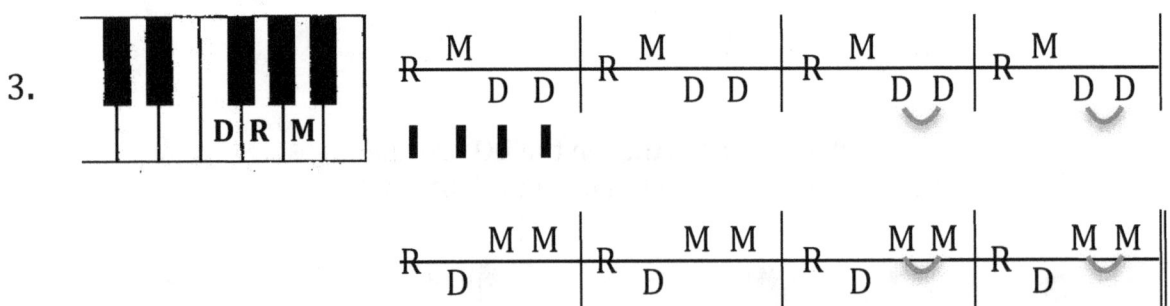

1st Challenge: Use tonal solfege to play and sing each exercise.
2nd Challenge: Play using different left hand finger sets.

LESSON 14 (major tonality melodies)

Major tonality - a quality of sound created when DO is the *resting tone* or *tonic*. When played, **major tonality** typically evokes feelings of happiness, excitement, or joy. When a composer picks notes from the major pattern to write a song, then the song will often evoke the same types of feelings. This is contrasted with *minor tonality* patterns which can sound sad or reflective.

Transpose - to play a song using a DO other than the one shown.

  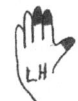

Mary Had A Little Lamb

 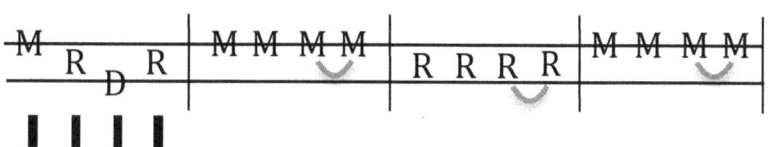

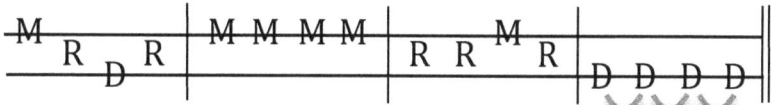

Coronation

Oliver Holden (1765-1844)

 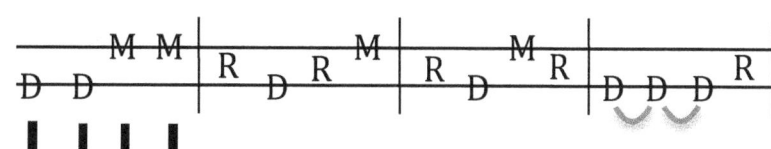

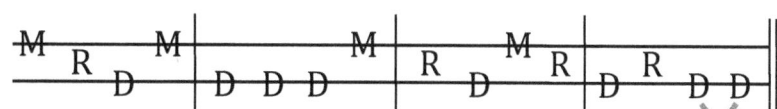

1st Challenge: Use tonal solfege to play and sing.
2nd Challenge: Transpose to a different white key DO.
3rd Challenge: Transpose to a black key DO.

LESSON 15 (DRM notation)

In this book the location of DO on a staff is shown by a DO block ■

Sometimes DO is on a LINE: Sometimes DO is in a SPACE:

Right Hand
Play the following exercises using different right hand finger combinations.

1.  Half Note Macrobeat. The starting note is DO.

2.  Quarter Note Macrobeat. The starting note is DO.

1st Challenge: Play line 1 and 2 with your left hand.
2nd Challenge: Play line 1 hands together.
3rd Challenge: Play line 2 using *dynamics*. Which *dynamics* did you choose?

Left Hand

Play the following exercises using different left hand finger combinations.
Use excellent hand position and playing technic.
The starting note may or may not be DO.

3. Quarter Note Macrobeat. *(RE and MI are a black keys.)*

4. Dotted Quarter Note Macrobeat. Use legato arm movement.

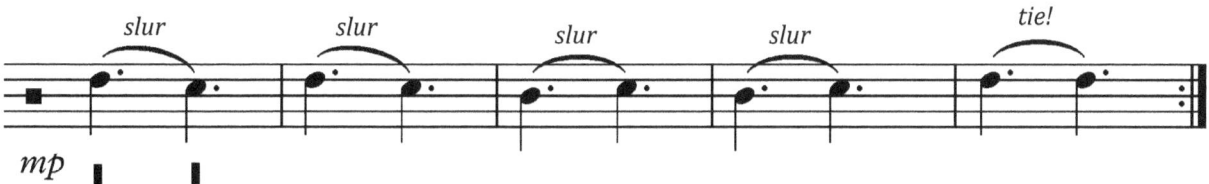

5. Quarter Note Macrobeat.

1st Challenge: Transpose line 4 up one whole-step and play again.
2nd Challenge: Sing and play line 5. Use tonal solfege.

35

186,000mps

This song uses DRM. Which fingers will you use?

Mark Swope

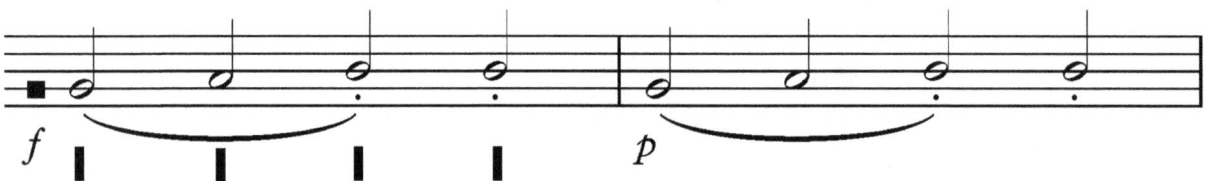

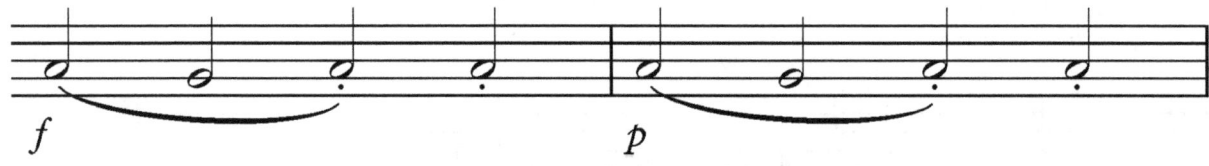

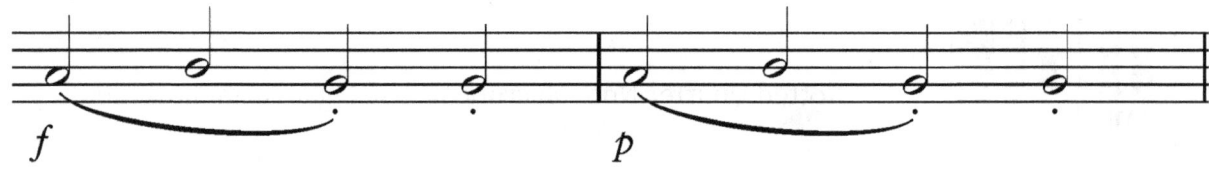

1st Challenge: Play simultaneously with both hands.
2nd Challenge: Sing using solfege while you play.
3rd Challenge: Play hands together with the RH in a high location and LH in a low location.

LESSON 16 (grand staff)

Grand Staff – Two staffs (or staves) used at the same time. The top staff is for high notes and the bottom staff is for low notes. They are connected by a curved bracket. When using the Grand Staff your eyes will need to notice both staffs at the same time, moving quickly back and forth from one to the other! When notes are written on top of each other (vertically) they are played at the same time.

Parallel Motion – when notes being played in both hands are moving in the same direction.

1. Parallel Motion. (Half Note Macrobeat.) Using DRM.
  Decide which fingers you will use. Try different finger combinations.

2. Parallel Motion (Dotted Quarter Note Macrobeat).

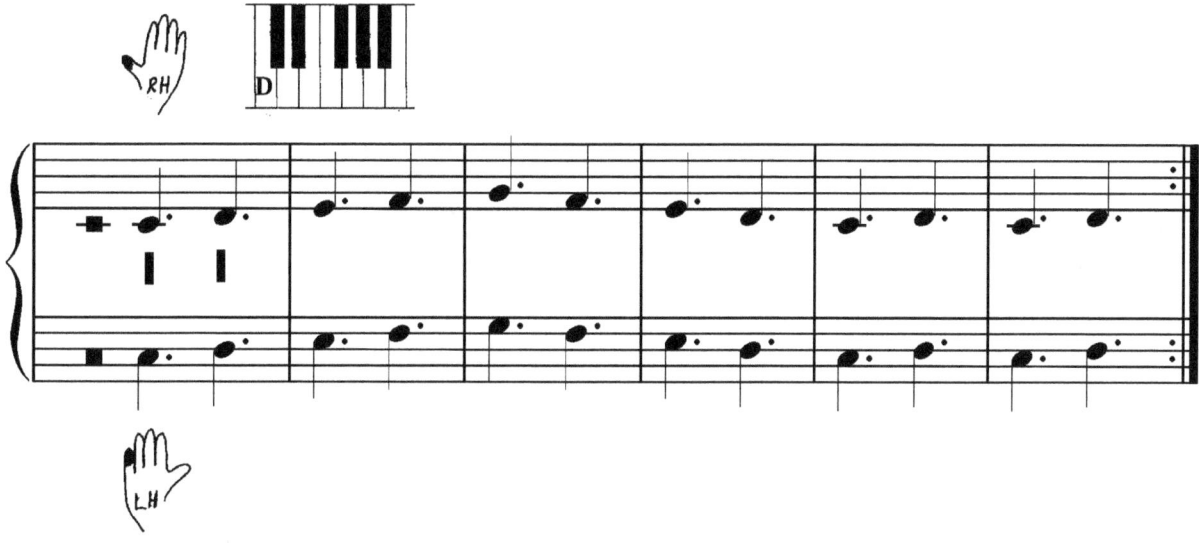

Challenge: Transpose exercise 1 to a black key DO and play again.

#Rainbows

This song uses DRM. Which fingers will you use?

Mark Swope

Score Analysis
1. What is the title?
2. Who is the composer?
3. What dynamics are used?
4. Which articulation is used?

5. What kind of note gets the macrobeat?
6. How many beats in each measure?
7. What is the form of this piece?

1st Challenge: Transpose to a black key DO and play again.
2nd Challenge: Using the original DO, sing and play using solfege.
3rd Challenge: Use different finger combinations in both hands.
4th Challenge: Transpose to a different DO and play again.

> Generally, legato is used when there is no articulation marking.

Strudel

This song uses DRM. Which fingers will you use?

Ian Kirk

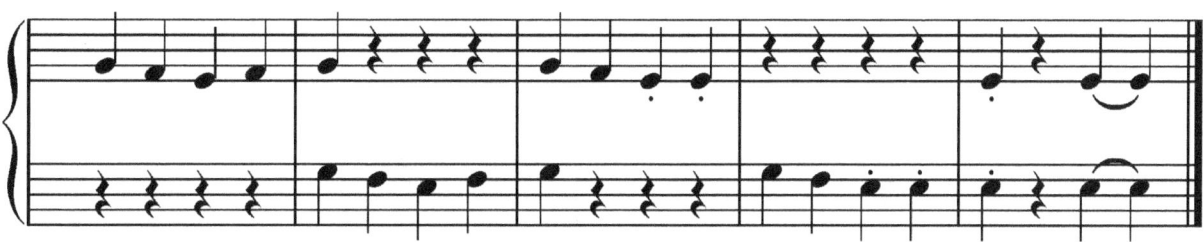

Score Analysis:
1. What is the title?
2. Who is the composer?
3. Which hand plays the *statement*?
4. Which hand plays the *repetition*?
5. What articulations are used?
6. What dynamic did you choose?

1st Challenge: Transpose to a different white key DO.
2nd Challenge: Transpose to a black key DO.
3rd Challenge: Use different finger sets in both hands.
4th Challenge: Add microbeat rhythms to some of the beats.

Theme - The statement of a musical idea.

Variation - The retelling of a *theme* with some changes. A theme can be followed by one or more variations.

1st Challenge: Create a 2nd variation by playing the theme with hands in different locations.
2nd Challenge: Create another variation by transposing the theme.
3rd Challenge: Create another variation by adding microbeat rhythms to the theme.

LESSON 17 (treble and bass clefs)

 The Treble Clef is a 9th century symbol that represents the high sounds of the piano, and appears on the top staff. Treble means "third" because it was used to identify the third voice part (soprano) in 14th century music. The <u>Treble Clef</u> generally represents **high** notes from the center of the keyboard and up.

 The Bass Clef is a 9th century symbol that represents the low sounds of the piano, and appears on the bottom staff. Bass means "low sounds" and was used to identify the lowest of musical sounds beginning in the 14th century. The <u>Bass Clef</u> generally represents **low** notes from the center of the keyboard and down.

Rocking the Dog

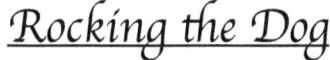

Steadily

Mark Swope

LESSON 18 (LTD tonal solfege)

LA (Lah) - a starting tone in solfege. LA can be the *resting tone*, or *tonic*. LA can be any key on the keyboard. Music notation will always indicate which key is DO and which key is LA.

Minor Tonality - a flavor of sound that is typically sad or reflective. When DO is the resting tone then the tonality is *major*. When LA is the resting tone then the tonality is *minor*.

Any key can be LA

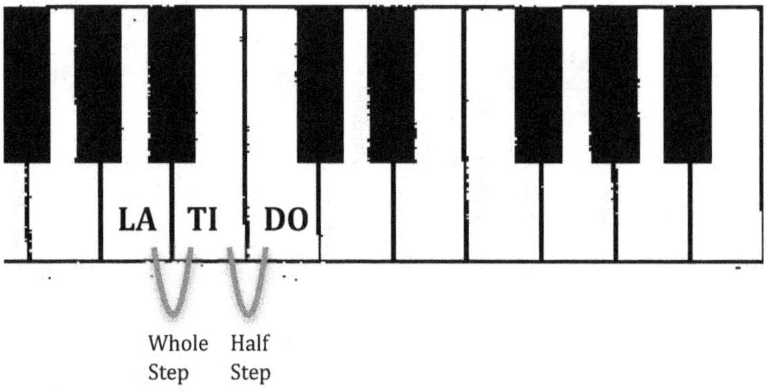

Example 1 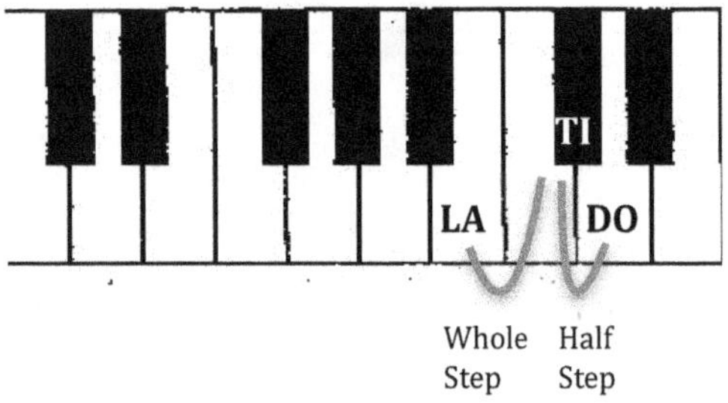   Example 2

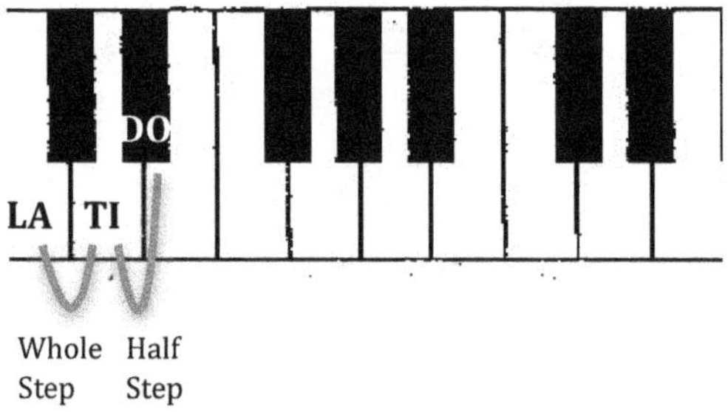

Play DTL starting on the DO provided. Use different sets of fingers.

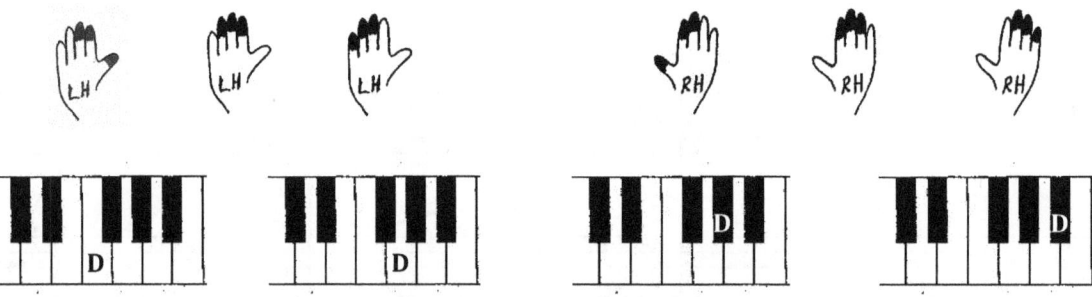

Red Light, Green Light

1.

Song Analysis
1. Measures 1-2 create Pattern A. How many times is Pattern A heard?
2. Which two measures are different than Pattern A? This is Pattern B.
3. What is the musical form of *Red Light, Green Light*?

1st Challenge: Sing and play using tonal solfege.
2nd Challenge: Play using different right hand fingers.

I Lost My Shoe

2.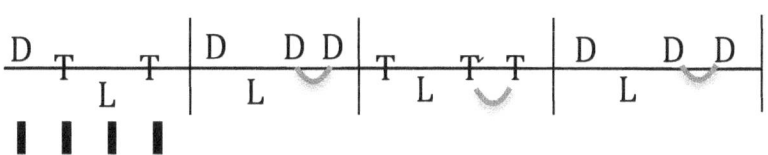

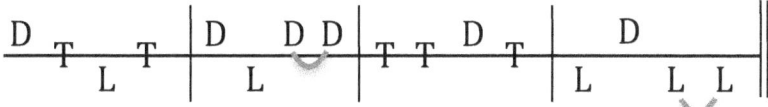

Song Analysis
1. Which measures of the first line are the same as the second? Which are different?
2. Does *I Lost My Shoe* sound major or minor?

1st Challenge: Sing and play using tonal solfege.
2nd Challenge: Play with the left hand. Which fingers will you use?

LESSON 19 (minor solfege melodies)

Play each song starting with the finger shown.

 *Rose Thorn, Why Do You Scorn?* (L T D)

1.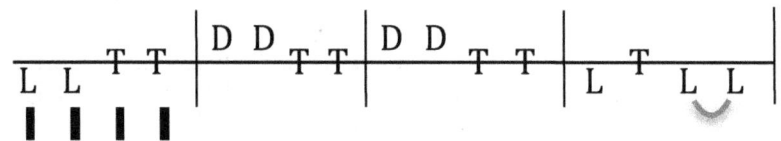

 Mushy Cereal (L T D R)

2.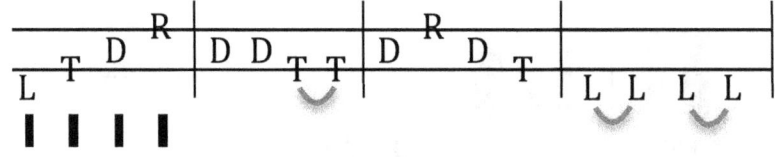

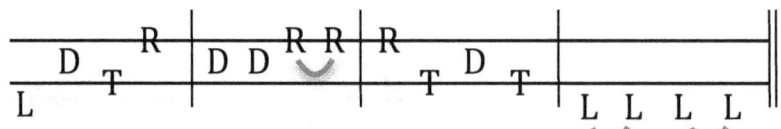

1st Challenge: Play each song using different right hand fingers.
2nd Challenge: Transpose each piece (move DO).
3rd Challenge: Sing and play using tonal solfege.

LESSON 20 (LTD notation)

The location of DO on a staff is shown by a DO block ■   Even though the tonality is minor – and LA is the resting tone - the DO Block still indicates DO.

1st Challenge: Play with the LH in a very low location.
2nd Challenge: Play using different sets of fingers.
3rd Challenge: Play this song as if the title is "Fireworks!" How is the song played differently?

45

Appendix A (major pentachords)

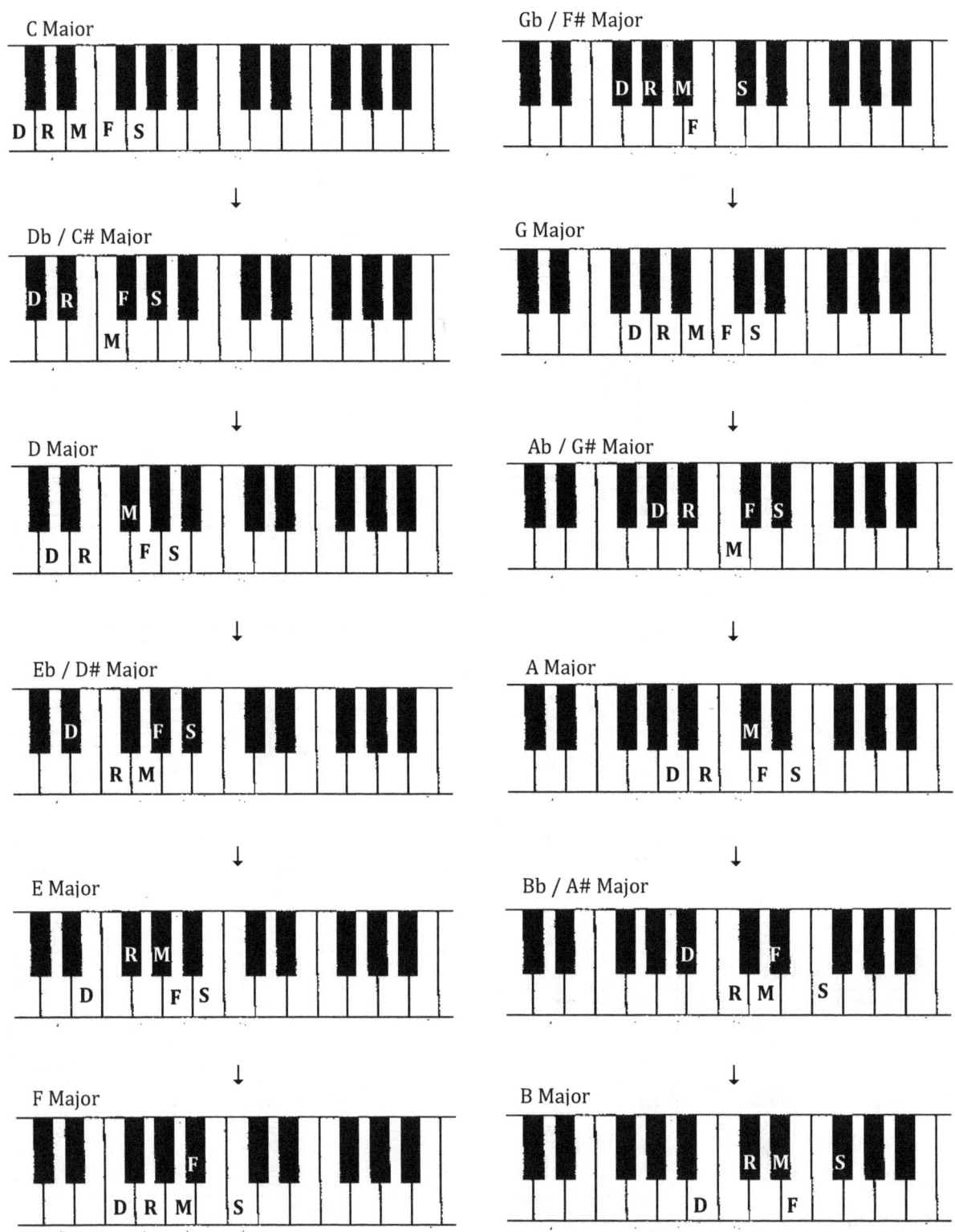

Appendix B (minor pentachords)

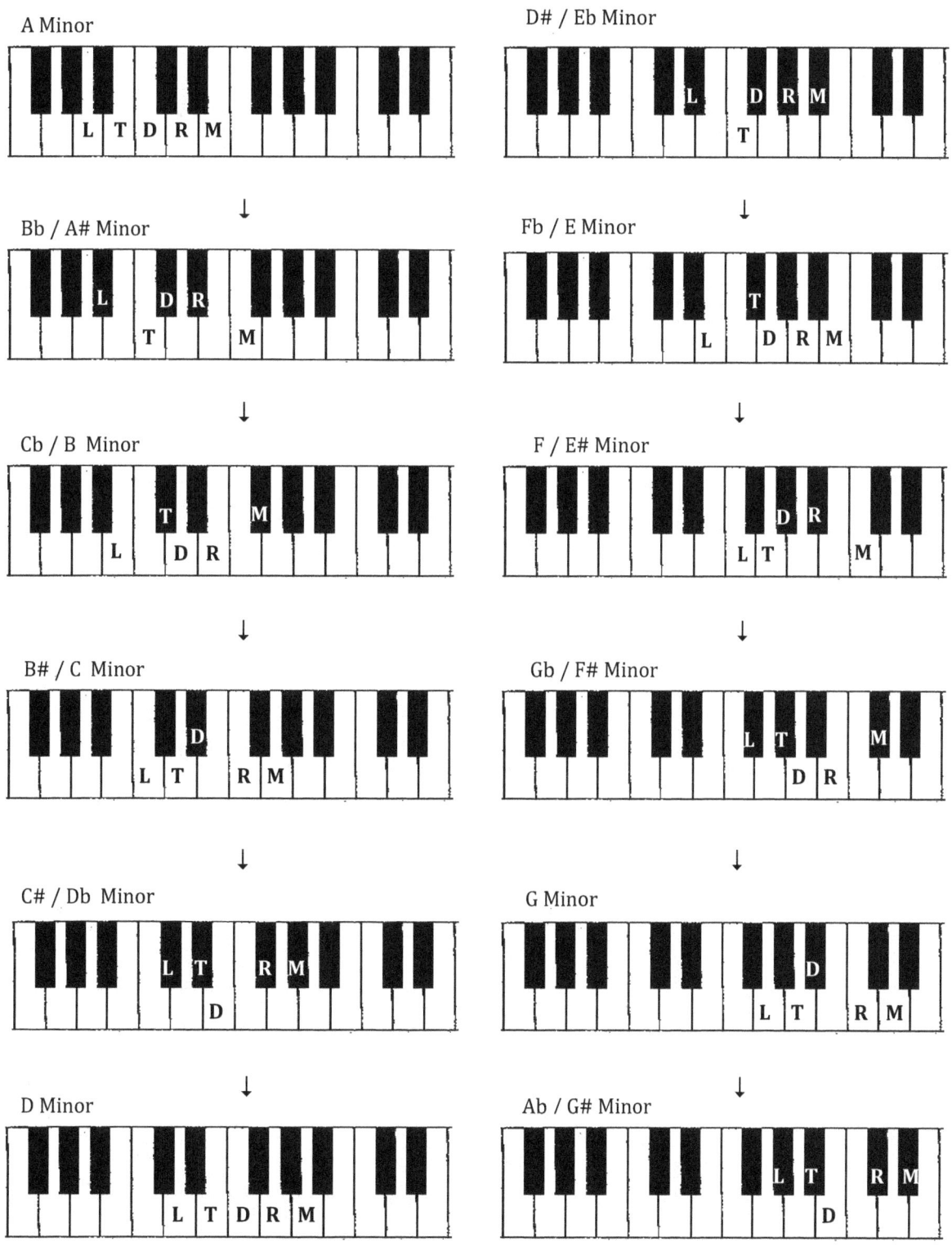

$12.95
ISBN 978-1-7323086-0-2

www.ingramcontent.com/pod-product-compliance
Lightning Source LLC
Chambersburg PA
CBHW081330040426
42453CB00013B/2366